RE:VERSES

CHRIS CAMPANIONI & KRISTINA MARIE DARLING

the operating system c. 2019

the operating system digital print//document

RE:VERSES

ISBN # 978-1-946031-63-1
copyright © 2019 by Chris Campanioni and Kristina Marie Darling
edited and designed by ELÆ [Lynne DeSilva-Johnson] with Orchid Tierney

is released under a Creative Commons CC-BY-NC-ND (Attribution, Non Commercial, No Derivatives) License: its reproduction is encouraged for those who otherwise could not afford its purchase in the case of academic, personal, and other creative usage from which no profit will accrue.

Complete rules and restrictions are available at:
http://creativecommons.org/licenses/by-nc-nd/3.0/

For additional questions regarding reproduction, quotation, or to request a pdf for review contact operator@theoperatingsystem.org

Print books from The Operating System are distributed to the trade by SPD/Small Press Distribution, with ePub and POD via Ingram, with production by Spencer Printing, in Honesdale, PA, in the USA. Digital books are available directly from the OS, direct from authors, via DIY pamplet printing, and/or POD.

This text was set in Steelworks Vintage, Europa-Light, Gill Sans, Minion, and OCR-A Standard.

Cover Art uses an image from "Collected Objects & the Dead Birds I Did Not Carry Home," by Heidi Reszies.

the operating system
www.theoperatingsystem.org
mailto: operator@theoperatingsystem.org

RE:VERSES

RE: VERSE (ON THE FUTURE OF COLLABORATIVE POETICS & ANONYMITY)
CHRIS CAMPANIONI & KRISTINA MARIE DARLING

Long before the Internet was re-routed from military servers and then mainstreamed, Michel Foucault understood the efficacy of anonymous interactions on the level of literature, imagining a culture where discourse would circulate without any need for an author. But what he was asking in 1969 is something we can better answer today, because it seems less germane to call into question the need for an author in a culture in which everyone is writing, producing, and reproducing text, and more effective to think about re-evaluating the notion of a single author, or what it means to *write by yourself*. But it isn't enough to say I am sitting here, alone, at my dinner table which I so often use for writing, as I type this, and yet in constant communication and communion with all of you, so many of whom I will never know. One would have to testify to the particular medium we have at our disposal, the actual discourse of the Internet, its ultimate permissibility, its provocations for collaboration and co-creation. One would have to surrender the idea that authors own anything besides our will to keep producing, and our desire for change; and to modulate means to resist without negating, to alter without omitting, to enable something new to come forward: unfolding of the text into the anonymity of a murmur.

And really it isn't the Internet which has fostered these ideas of collaborative authorship but the classical world. We already know that for the ancients, every act of creation comes from elsewhere, something unformed or uncompleted, which was *made to grow*. It's why "to author" all the way down to its Latin roots signifies advising, witnessing, *and* transferring. It's why to author something means to also forget the act of saying "I," to forget it or to make it recede in the background in service of the other or others, on behalf of a community, for the sake of an audience.

When I think of collaborative poetics I often think about the poetics of relation, and thinking about what it means to be directly in contact with everything possible, an always-open structure in which, as Glissant said, "the creator of a text is effaced, or rather, is done away with, to be revealed in the texture of his creation." When a solid melts, it reveals something always underneath, something at the very bottom, something inside—something new and something that was *always already there*. What I want is the intimacy of anonymous encounters within the text itself, and yet to be effaced and revealed, even and especially by my own authorial departure. And it would take the form of a repetition or a reversal; a re: verse in which we correspond lyrically; a re: verse in which our correspondence becomes the poem.

Of course, an integral part of any correspondence is the space between things, those slender apertures lit up with waiting. It is in these liminal spaces that possibility accumulates. We write toward this space, in response to its silences.

Because we are neither here nor there, the rules of syntax and grammar, and their implicit logic, no longer hold. More specifically, liminal spaces offer the possibility of new causal relationships. Which is to say, *after this* no longer means *because of this*. Since we are in no man's land, working at the periphery of the governing bodies associated language, it becomes difficult if not impossible to enforce any normative idea about how language, and narrative, for that matter, should behave.

Nota bene: the meaning of the word aperture is twofold: 1.) a hole or gap. 2.) a space through which light passes in an optical or photographic instrument, particularly the variable opening by which light enters a camera.

A collaboration functions in much the same way, capturing radiance as it passes from one person's fingertip to the next.

In a recent interview on their co-written volume, John Gallaher and G.C. Waldrep refer to this interstitial space, and the light that fills its corridors, as the "third voice," belonging to both practitioners and neither one of them. Because there is no textual ownership, per se, it becomes difficult to hold someone accountable, let alone take up the customary practices surrounding language usage: copyright, attribution, citation. It is no coincidence that these routine procedures are bound up with questions of value, and the economies in which texts circulate. By abandoning the single-author text, we create a space outside of (or beyond) the linguistic marketplace.

———

One way we can think of this "third voice" is by thinking of glossolalia, this biblical "speaking in tongues" which also represents the generally ungraspable, a polylinguistic discourse which can't be conquered or claimed; which exists, in fact, to disrupt the persistent motion *to grasp*. And to grasp is to understand, but before that, it is the attempt to hold, to have, to own. "How can a living being have language?" Agamben asks. I would return: Is it not, instead, language which has a living being? To the extent that language turns one into an "I" through the act of becoming, a move into subjectification and desubjectification, the unrepeatable and its repetition, within the trauma of enunciation, *so to speak*, or to begin to understand what cannot be spoken. The poetics of collaboration speaks in that silence, that call or signal, coded with repetition and cessation, the pause before another voice returns, a track resumes, a word is placed behind a blinking black dash, if you are doing this at your laptop and we are. And elsewhere

A message in my inbox provides me with WHAT'S NEW IN YOUR GROUP: When does a poem stop being yours? I don't click here to View Discussion; I don't click out. I begin to Add a comment, which becomes this project, this process of turning off so as to turn the page: a conversation and conversion, but also a returning to the primacy of the event of language, whose power is located in being almost unlocatable. The point is not to know what happens next, as in any good writing, but to take it further; to resist the authorial urge to answer, to close things off, to finish. Part of this is in knowing the unknowable outside the frame; to relish and relinquish what can't be seen by just your own camera-eye. To think of the kitchen table when no one is looking—but more than that, to think of the kitchen table when one has photographed the parlor. Another way of saying this: it is always the unsayable which calls one to speak. When there is more than one voice, we must imagine one another's silences as if they are our own.

———

The house grows quiet again. We are unsure who is at the door, and who has already passed through the silver gates. In the parlor, there is a single painting displayed on a white wall. A beige canvas that reads:

> THIS PAINTING IS A PROPOSAL. I PROPOSE WE MEET
> ONCE A YEAR UNTIL ONE OF US CAN'T OR WON'T.

Of course, the obvious question: in that year, filled with works and days, where does the mind travel, and with whom?

In the age of virtual reproduction, most collaborations take place over vast expanses of landscape and weather. The voice on the other end of the receiver could be anyone, not just the dark-eyed girl standing in a garden, holding a plucked flower in her profile pic. It is what we don't know, and cannot yet know, that pulls us farther into a forest of bright and burning branches. Here, fact becomes limitation, inscribing the boundaries of what is possible. It is more liberating not to know.

That silence is the struck match, the last light.

———

2017-2018

Strange to think of machines that way
I know the cold
Grip of confidence or how
A forgetting must
Also be erotic   How I have
Always reached for a body
Made to last
The fall   I am told
& I am still telling this
As cars part
Route 4 into
Soft focus   A point
Of Google Earth
I've already reproduced
From habit—I'm here
Again—A stretch
Of skin folding
Inward like prayers
Into a waiting palm
No one is expecting
Me for days or else
I've forgotten who I am
I can still
See myself there

Dangling like oranges
In grove   I am the first
Person to make
Eye contact
All night   Rain
Sliding across my cheek
To cut my copy
Like a secret
River   A choice
To remember or erase
Some people
Watch me & want to
Fall in love a second
Time   I want
To say something
Always survives this
Being what we
Call a witness

7:37 PM
Sunday, December 23

When I begin the story
the question of power
seems inevitable   I don't
know how to open that box
can't seem to turn the key
without breaking it apart
I want to keep driving
in the same way I want
to tell you the truth
& still be able to look at you
straight on   At night
the felled trees
the telephone
wires a field of dead
aster that goes on
for miles   Which is
to say: I am a lit
match & I'm trying to
keep myself from turning
up the heat
You see, there are only two
kinds of weather
Yes, the storm
sirens are pitched

at a higher frequency
& now the same
dream   You are standing
there with the book
in your hand
saying over & over
I thought I knew you

8:09 PM
Sunday, December 23

The storm, the book, the dream
The key, the match, the box

The heat   The poem
Is teaching me something

To say I have
Missed myself again   Too

Often wanting only
Something to hold up

The time it takes to hang
A copy & let it dry

In the dark   How I can
Know & even believe

I can't help
But to move or to keep

From moving   I
Read in absence

Of the body as a ritual
The Greeks would burn

A wooden double
Of the deceased

Instead   They called
Me a colossus

11:29 AM
Tuesday, December 26

But there are
other exhibits in that
museum: the final
room was the site
of the real violence
& the annex still
belongs to a dead
woodsman: trophy
after motionless
trophy You see,
even trained
falcons wear
blinders during
the hunt At the end
of the corridor
you'll find the next
dispatch This is when
you forget
about the locked
box, the field,
the snow.
You realize
as the unease
blossoms beneath

your skin
you realize
you will need
the match

4:16 PM
Tuesday, December 26

Some strange

        Voices aren't

Clear before

                My conversion

      Gone wrong

Kind of

                  Me

The same

        Who needs that

Control

        Who needs that

                  To understand

        Why I remember all

The lines

                  I should say

      Your face

Counts

        The beats

        As in a treatment

Our thin film
>	Feeling

Me up
>	Again

6:10 PM
Thursday, December 28

Of course, there's more than one way to burn a building down. Even now, you're imagining what we've only seen in films: Cadillac crashing into an air conditioning unit, a woman in a white dress telephoning the ambulance driver. What I've been trying to say, failing to say, is this: control is the first harbor, the last ship. So, I gather the objects you've tossed into the street. The ruined tablecloth and the broken dish.

The single-serving spoon, glittering in the dry heat.

6:27 PM
Thursday, December 28

There was a lot of talk about
Night sweats my pumping
Grip a group

Of white men wondering
Whether sex addiction
Is a real thing

On the screen
When does a poem stop
Being yours?

One dream   To be
A person
Illustrated with images

Of the moment
Style   Industry   Fashion   Daytime
TV   The pictures   A boy   A beehive

& so on   (Any center
Of movement)   Intended to make
Me look at any cost & look

Good on a page
I've paused before
A kind of form

For being identical with every
Day life   What you
Call a child's nervous

Energy   How utterly
Flush as a thumbnail
Breaks open with just

A touch & back to
The humming wait   Nothing
If not the whimper

My body makes soon
As I rise—the same
As ever   Of all the tongues

I had I had only
Understood the words of one
& half the words

Of another   Coming out
Of order like a bad dub
How it felt to be tossed

Into language   To know
So clearly without having
To know why   To still

Hear the words sounding
Like wet hair   Put on
Like the warmth

Of a dinner party
Or the cool clarity of death
In knowing this

Was never only mine

8:39 PM
Wednesday, January 3

In the lyceum, the lecture on property rights goes on & on. A man is standing at the podium, tapping its embossed surface with a dull pencil. A hush falls over the room, & he begins to speak:

Close your eyes & turn to any page in the book. Place your finger on the text. The sentence you have trapped with the work of your hands, this is your answer. Now open your eyes, & do not look away from what you have chosen.

So I come to & the declaration is written in a strange language:

Bonjour, tristesse. Je ne sais pas un autre mot.....

Around me, the reception has already begun. An entire room of older men, holding champagne flutes & paper napkins, telling me to smile. So I bare my perfect teeth. I look to my left

10:57 AM
Friday, January 5

to come to come to   to look so long so as to   become
the thing you look at   it is sometime since   I have been
myself & I don't   mind or pay for   an exact translation

to the french   I can't pronounce un autre mot   google gives all
the things I am   any way passing through papers   paper
sons & paper daughters   (I can hear their footsteps in place

of my own)   what careful choreography   can move
bodies with just a slip   permission to feel
like   a natural woman   man son daughter   & citizen

hello sadness   I don't know another word for this kind
passage between   nations & time   under one
roof & yet within an orchard   to walk through the living

rooms of other people's childhoods & to play their gazes   the short & long hands   their voices   over mine   reciting this as the guide directs our tour elsewhere

eat blessings eat all that is forbidden   I can feel the sun in my mouth

I can feel the eyes on my eyes   life   owes me nothing

5:06 PM
Monday, January 8

still when passing through customs   most men insist they are owed:
a loaded gun   a beveled mirror   a beautiful girl
check all that apply   once you've answered there is no way to unmark the paper
only a slight tremor   in the throat gives   away a lie
think fast   do you feel terror first in the face or in the hands
the reason I'm asking   only one of us can have a key   to the fireproof safe
I need to know you   won't strike the match too soon
I realize I haven't the right   I waited for you by the gate
but left with *le jardinière* when you were detained at the airport   *c'est terrible alors*
the walk into the city went on   & on until my looking   became conspicuous
after all   the word *spectacle*   comes from the Latin
   spectaculum
meaning "a public show"   is there a woman if no one's standing there looking

11:34 PM
Monday, January 8

soothe the flesh & quiet the mind   like words

into a well   descending as they distort   my instructor

saying softly if your eyes   wander your body will wander too & I

wonder about the reality of kitchen tables   (my left palm in between

my right knee, my right arm unfolded)   how often the act

of conditioning can be erotic   (the damp skin, the head

bowed lightly, all of this   under a jetting stream   but one should have

to wait for it)   so in the end it became all   a matter of moving

a tree toward the middle

thinking all the time

how many people are thinking

of me as I think of this

my favorite scene being

the time Lily with only one

L pictures the beautiful
boots walking themselves

into the bedroom
that is to say husked of subject
that is to say clothing
without a body is there

a more beautiful
image than the space where one
has been   or where one might
otherwise be placed

10:25 AM
Wednesday, January 10

While you are taking inventory, counting the straps on her boots, they've already begun the auction. Needless to say, you didn't realize the gravity of the summons, those crumpled papers their lawyers served us with last week, the way old debts always come due. At the podium, the bald man in his three-piece suit appraises the chandelier at $455,790.00 even. What to do when no one bids on the thing you loved most—

A long silence, a bit of music. They roll the little cart back to the stockroom. If a bobby pin won't fit in the lock, a trial seems inevitable. Supposing broken glass is found in the corridor, here is some money for your defense, a key to the judge's chambers. Inside the cabinet clearly marked with your name

there are some things you don't need to see.

9:47 PM
Thursday, January 18

A book that begins
The CIA can neither confirm nor deny the existence or nonexistence of record
responsive to your request

A book that begins on applause

A book that begins on what it is you are writing (outside) the text

(If you see something, say something)

I keep waiting for you to take
Over, to move & so to move
The story beyond itself

I this, I that

The President tells a reporter
Who is kind enough to listen

That is
To say
Who is kind enough to ask

(Whatever is written down I read out loud & whatever I hear I write down)

I wanted this to resemble nothing but itself: A book that begins
As a mirror

Think everybody think: closed-circuit video feeds

Are not for prospective shop-lifters but
Prosaic clerks working the shop floor

The ritual breaking
Down of a body to be
Reassembled elsewhere

(They called it "participatory monitoring")

A discussion on what it is "like" to be [　] within the terms of the
mode of being human
Specific to our "present moment"

(These are the records, files, time sheets, documents, photographs,
bodily data, image & text sequences that together form a flow chart
of the modern subject)

The body as a born recorder

CLICK   CLICK   CLICK

We can open me up later &
Extract the film

Think everybody think

The most strategic element of surveillance is not its subject's certain lack of evasion but the uncertainty over whether or not one is ever being surveilled. (Some people like to

                                      Say:) You feel me. There is

no grip harder than the one which can't be held. This is
                                  The difference between a
handshake & any act of aggression on behalf of a guilty party

(In this paradigm, "North America" may be used in place of "a guilty party")

They called it "categorical suspicion"

They called it "material compression"

Which is to say there is more than one way
To sort things out

To repeat
A long silence, a bit of music, &

(By "things" they meant bodies)

9:55 PM
Friday, January 18

Then there are the { } that cannot—will not—be named. I tried to phone you, but the burning building went on & on. Room after room of ruined photographs, a bright threshold waiting behind the plain wall.

Which is to say: I saw what was on the film reel only after it had caught fire:

There was no graceful way to strike the match, let alone leave money at a scorched altar. You were the first payout, the last debt. Now the envelope is too hot to touch.

In the double mirror, I see you trying to control the duration of that fire's heat. You must understand, there are types of weather that don't have a switch, that aren't wired to a closed circuit.

Listen when I tell you: the body is no machine.

4:47 PM
Thursday, January 25

Unspeakable, unutterable, ineffable—a building on fire: thou shalt not be seen.
Which is to say euphemism. Which is to say unmentionables. Which is to say *the
forbidden words are*

a fetus of transition   the gift of a body
becoming   who can make
out & with what evidence-based consent
that every word even now was
meant to rise? I was

satisfied with my body   I took
pleasure in the entitlement of my own
rich diversity   to have this name
my own vulnerable flesh   my eyes   our color
changing even now

this sometimes
smile   determined not to discompose
myself before committing
these thoughts to print
how even poetry can be a science

based on the biological need
to pass   to amble unmercifully
urged on toward the new
pledge to resist & to
measure this

                                  resistance by remembering
                              the state-sanctioned disappearance
                               of unwonted persons   all those
                                       bodies for whom to be
                                          forbidden is not

                                          a curse but in fact
                                              a reckoning
                                         to flee toward one's own
                                         disappearance as a form
                                              of refuge

                    Transgendered & transnational & to be. To be

Beyond words could also mean to be after them. To come into them. Out-cast. Undesirables & indésirables. What is the sense of turning words into a god, to adore in silence. What is the sense of not feeling the heat rising through one's own body. What is the sense. The reel missing from the film begins with a voice-over against the purple-pink swath of the dying sun. I am asking you to move me higher

2:14 PM
Friday, January 26

What I've meaning to say, and failing to say, is this: I'm afraid of heights. You see, there are only two types of women: the girls who are more like honey, and the ones who are bright & beveled glass, hoarding what's inside. You keep asking what the metaphor means, that real thing that the gloved hand is reaching for, spreading its thin fingers in the falling snow. All I can say is {   } which of course is no help when you're trying to load a gun—

Before the staircase, before the housefire, before each word became unsayable, I called you from the airport, but you didn't pick up. You were the first dial-tone, the longest silence.

Can you even hear me, asking impossible questions from twelve stories above:

Well, take a few days to think it over. In the meantime: I need to know what made it through customs, and whether the fireproof safe, in fact, lit up beneath a heap of ash.

1:12 PM
Saturday, January 27

To suppose, to lay down tentatively, to hold, to have a position of, to say
I did it for the fantasy, & for the memory, & for the viewers across the
screen (the viewers out there) … there are certain faces

There are certain moments in the underground

There are certain expressions I'd like to see in the underground, on the
faces of the passengers moving through me just as I am moving

Through the city, for pleasure & for passage, & for the inevitable pause
within a station's stop, the rasping announcement, the cessation of
composition (a moment

In which I am forced to stop composing, so as to get off, unless I delay

My own arc, to stay on & ride another) Not to be
The bullet but the shot—

The city, the boredom, the beautiful body of being at the same time

Over & under everything

(I stay on & keep

Moving; I even

Repeat myself, once
More turning
Fantasy into memory into a view
To a kill: it is my only
True dependency)

What I wouldn't do to re-live the last moment from the tomorrow of today, to see the face at the height of climax, an expression of shock & disgust & sure silence; an empty expression; a face emptied-out of all thought & feeling, to be filled in or up again later, saying softly it is what it is I am what I am & you remember hope of a new feeling strange flesh the mouth & lips dim room pants rip quick & silent coming another scene in the shallow end where I am still waiting, I am still waiting, I am still waiting to

Descend becoming what it was I would
Never be some unspoken
Satisfaction where there is a pause, hold
The pause   I would like you
To keep going

First thing I look for is my own face in the mirror of others for want is said
& want is said in so many ways

2:45 PM
Saturday, January 27

[PART SECOND] I am trying to explain to you
the difference between a bullet and a shot: it's not
the velocity, but the impact of one body striking
the other. A tear at the edge of the tablecloth is the first
sign that violence also lives in this set of rooms, its presence
made visible in the (   ) that appear
in each of your textbooks, the faces of dead presidents
filled with light. Which to say: there are men who overuse
the word pleasure & they are easy to pick out in a crowd—

Of course, when we started making the film, we didn't know. The audience was smaller then. & no one had taken their first steps into the underground, let alone a walk to the train station at night, stuttering in the empty street.

Now the script goes on & on. What comes first, the feature film in the mind or the film outside of it. Take your time answering. Remember to bring a bouquet for that woman who assembled each of your elaborate two-story sets.

& I shouldn't have to remind you: When plucking a flower, no one keeps the thorn.

3:25 PM
Saturday, January 27

Feeling a little
Like Orpheus except
We were meant to
Look back
As is our nature

Do men grow
Gay with age
I think as I
Bring one's eyes into
My gaze, nothing turns

Me on like my
Morning suffocation
Still I want to
Talk about the two
Story set, the station

At night, the pleasure
Of picking you out
In a crowd, all the violence
Done in the name of
This stuttering flesh

(They paid to have the scene run backward)   In the dark, in the middle
Of day like

The tempo of a good film, a moving neon sign provided by the puddle reflecting it on asphalt

(The city could be anywhere) You don't need to know

Who steps in when
I step out

4:39 PM
Sunday, January 28

& I didn't think you wanted to know about the man who followed me from the metro stop, how we only seemed to be meeting for the first time.

He wouldn't tell me where we were going, let alone the color of his second wife's hair. Abigail, Luisa, Meg. The names of women started to accumulate, a heap of flowers in which I would eventually drown—

Needless to say, the space between his mouth and mine bore the weight of it all: the plucked rose, the bouquet, the notes you slipped beneath my door. The envelope & its scorched papers.

Days later, he's still stammering about the time he touched my hair, blue dress trailing from the platform. You see, there's a way I can leave a room without even getting out of my chair.

Now that you're listening, the same question is burning at the back of my throat. Now I'm looking up from the dictionary, now I'm raising my hand—

7:03 PM
Thursday, February 1

but I never cut the other

        kites   & since   then I

recall how I was   made

        me kneel with my

facing outward

                a pail full

dark   sky   not to mention

other things   & my two hands

    designed to be flown

pressed together   & seeing that

I could get some air

        the same to me

as to the others

  again to what

  question was already covered

    facing outward &

  forced my head down   without my

  knowing just as I was

  a long string

  about to

      cloth or plastic

   come closer to me

  I shook

  my half-carried

  to leave something like that

    as above an altar

   unreturned

      & to start to see

             how another was standing

in for

                    my body (one

always reads

            just as I was about to

too much

            breathe deeper

into things)

            it is always

a question of

            cutting   & this was

repeated again & again

            not to mention

my youth as far

    again & again

as my chest

    & called in another

again & again

    to accept the first part

(several times in a matter

    & personally took (a)part

of minutes to which

    held me with my feet up

I could only sing silently

    in the air

a hymn I had known by heart

    to try some other method

as a child)

    am I supposed to

        lie then

            on a bed of news

    papers   keeping

        to myself

        so to speak

(I was once again

        & this repeated

silent)

        thinking what's been left

out   what I can't

do you

        remember   after

syndication

after the careful

rendition

to be read

but I never

more than two

ways   cut

to a

question I

credit

sequence &

try & protect

the seething flesh

too large for the film

so as to never be

shown together in a single

shot

        this is what D&G

    call

      a *smooth space*

9:36 PM
Friday, February 2

The last time we met   in a garden near Bordeaux you would pause before speaking

The stutter & wait   a lit match passed between our teeth

Come closer to me   But I knew at that point you had thought it out

alone on the terrace the night before   when I thought you were busy loading the gun

when we will you understand   there is work to be done   the dead rarely cover their own tracks

What they cut from the film: wind snapping the string   a box-kite blazing into the field below

In the story aster meant   a spell but also   burning

épeler   there are some words you don't need   to know

What they didn't tell you: voice comes from outside the body   even it looks like I'm mouthing the words

2:32 PM
Saturday, February 3

& how I wondered what words could do, or even how
silence was at a time   the only way I could
have spoken   & how I
wondered then, repeating the same words I so often
announced as a child   my eyes
are tired my head is loose when would I really need
no one else in the room   to believe it   I fear you
like I fear myself the certain uncertainty of opening
up   as any other body in which I've slid
above or below   the hide
I've prepared for use   to save
myself   from flight   or the impossibility of
evasion   to want even   to be present
at my own defacement   to collapse
into what I could never be if it were only me looking
something we have only ever had   a name for

10:41 AM
Tuesday, February 6

~~Dear Burning Building,~~

~~I've said too much about that night on the bridge. Now the storm sirens have sounded & other women know exactly who you are.~~

~~Dear Blunt Knife,~~

~~What I meant was: I'd rather not speak about the meadow. The funeral, with its brightly colored bouquet and rows of empty seats, was more than enough.~~

~~Dear Flung Trophy,~~

~~When you gestured at the liquor cabinet, I knew you were jealous of the other men. Of the course the inside of a mouth is dark.~~

Dear Desecrated Throne,

Right now, I can't

4:14 PM
Friday, March 30

The authors thank the editors and readers of the following publications, in which portions of this book, sometimes in different versions, appeared:

Gulf Coast,
The Laurel Review,
Jet Fuel Review,
and
Poetry International.

56

AFTER-WORDS

POSTMARK AND POSSIBILITY
A CONVERSATION WITH
CHRIS CAMPANIONI &
KRISTINA MARIE DARLING

Greetings! Thank you for talking to us about your process today! Can you introduce yourselves, in a way that you would choose?

CHRIS CAMPANIONI: *What a difficult question! I suppose I'm so used to having so many others speak for me, so maybe that's where I'll start? I write very often in the interstices between identities and genres. I often write as a response to a cultural displacement I've experienced since childhood as a first-gen American and the product of forced migrations, as well as the physical dislocation of working for many years in media and fashion and within an economy of images, and I find that the "hybrid" or uncategorizable form becomes an opportunity to find empowerment exactly in that fragmentation and fluidity. Writing without genre or generic markers allows me to imbue the work with a kind of excess and also to find or form a certain poetics of accumulation and relation with the text and also the reader.*

KRISTINA MARIE DARLING: *I write across, beyond, and in spite of genre categories. While all of my work utilizes the artistic repertoire of poetry, I'm interested in the ways that poetic language can be brought to bear on what have heretofore been envisioned as purely scholarly questions. For me, every text is an act of deconstruction, a response to all that language that came before one's own. Because I'm deeply invested in poetics as a vehicle for response, critical analysis, and documentary impulses, collaboration has become an integral part of my practice. When working with Chris, I was thrilled for the opportunity to engage with his work as both scholar and practitioner. I envision my contributions as lyric criticism about, extensions of, proliferations from, and hypothetical questions pertaining to Chris's poetics. For me, this is the most exciting possibility of poetics, to make an argument – and watch transformation happen – through the behavior of the language itself.*

How did you meet and become collaborators? What made you want to work together? How did this project, in particular, emerge and come into being?

CC: *We met in Los Angeles at AWP15. Kristina was editor of Black Ocean's* Handsome *and had published my work in the issue's most recent (and final) issue. As soon as we shook hands and introduced ourselves to one another, I knew that we'd be great friends but I could have never guessed that we'd be working together on a collaborative project only a few years later. Last winter, Kristina messaged me asking if I'd be up for engaging in a poetic exercise to keep us productive and to challenge ourselves. I've worked for several years as an editor of various literary and culture journals but I had never produced a co-written work. I agreed to her proposal and immediately sent her a poem. She sent one back almost hours later—as the manuscript testifies to—and* RE:Verses *was born.*

KMD: *I'm a longtime admirer of Chris's work, and part of what drew me to this collaboration was our shared interest in critical writing and scholarship. I have always believed that every poem is, at its heart, and act of reading, a response to -- and a deconstruction of -- the work that has come before one's own. Whereas critics in the traditional sense respond through content, poets respond through the behavior of the language itself. Going into this collaboration, I was excited because Chris is such an insightful critic, and his background in literary and cultural theory is truly impressive, as much so as his poetry and hybrid texts. This collaboration offered a wonderful opportunity to use the artistic repertoire of poetry as a vehicle for critical deconstructions of one another's work. I'm intrigued by the way our collaboration became almost like a work of creative literary criticism.*

Why are you a poet/writer/artist?

KMD: *I'm a creative practitioner because I want to create a better world. What better place to make change happen than the very foundations of society, language itself?*

CC: *A student asked me that the other day and I told them what I often tell people: I write because* I have to. *So sure, this frees me up in certain ways from thinking about the framing* of a work in terms of its potential to be circulated and the act of circulation in general, but it's also a lot less about freedom than survival.

When did you decide you were a poet/writer/artist (and/or: do you feel comfortable calling yourself a poet/writer/artist, what other titles or affiliations do you prefer/feel are more accurate)?

KMD: I'm not comfortable with the term poet, because I feel it is misleading. So many readers and practitioners think of poetry as merely autobiographical, an articulation of one's lived experience and the resulting point of view. And this variety of poetry usually comes in lineated stanzas. For me, the writer's job is to imagine, and to question received forms of discourse. To call myself a poet would foreclose the possibility of hybridity, collage, appropriation, and templates that are not germane to poetry. For me, this is where all of the exciting things happen – in the bright apertures, in the space between the things we feel certain about. This is what's especially exciting about Chris's work, and what made it so much fun to collaborate with him. The silences in his poems are just as fraught with emotion and complexity as the words themselves.

CC: Yeah, the thing that always attracted me to Kristina besides her talent as a writer was her enthusiasm for contributing to the creative and literary discourses of our community. She is not "just a writer" but a sensitive and perceptive reader and scholar. I find that I continually strive to perform in a similar role as both a multimedia artist working in text, video, and image but also an instructor and a researcher, engaging in literary and art criticism.

What's a "poet" (or "writer" or "artist") anyway? What do you see as your cultural and social role (in the literary / artistic / creative community and beyond)?

KMD: I'm excited and heartened by the way the role of the poet is becoming increasingly hybridized, encompassing not only writing but curatorial work, advocacy, and activism. In my own practice, editing and publishing work by others, and advocating for that work, has expanded my sense of what is possible in my own writing. After all, as Marianne Moore famously argued, the poem itself is a curatorial endeavor, a tiny museum filled with strange objects, linguistic artifacts, and silence. I think this is part of the reason Chris and I worked so well together. He's also an editor, and a colleague of mine at Tupelo Quarterly, so we brought a similarly curatorial sensibility to our chapbook project.

CC: I'd written about a year ago about poetry and empathy, and the role of the poet in an essay for The Brooklyn Rail called "The Poet as Caretaker" … and I think today, now more than ever, this is especially true. We are here to observe, which means to know, sure, but moreover, to notice. And recognition means not only seeing but really understanding, a groping toward understanding, which so often starts or ends, or starts and ends, by asking fundamental questions—of ourselves and others.

In RE:Verses you are working with processes of reversal, repetition, effacement, and partial reveal -- considering the liminal "apetures lit up with waiting" that grow out of correspondence. Can you speak more to this, or to other specific intentions or goals you had for the work? Whose voices or work were you looking to as inspiration, if any?

CC: *When I began conceptualizing the project we were each actively writing toward, I immediately thought of Glissant, and also Wolfgang Iser, particularly his theory of reader-text relationship—thinking all the time about the "virtual convergence" between a reader and a text which creates a literary work. In our project, I thought about re-contextualizing this dyadic relationship to include two authors who were no longer authors but active readers, reading and responding to one another through highly-specific (or highly-specified at least) moments. If I could do one thing differently, it would have been to also include that spatial element—where were we at each moment we decided to write each other back?—and what does that geography do to situate or conversely, upend the reader who approaches this collaborative, hybrid text?*

KMD: *I've always been intrigued by the tradition that links poetic voice and alterity. In other words, poetic voice is not our own, but instead, it is an otherness that speaks through us, and the poet is only the vessel. For Homer, this alterity was the muses, for H.D., it was the unconscious mind, for Jack Spicer, it was radio transmissions from outer space. And for many writers working in collaborative frameworks, this otherness is the "third voice" that emerges, which belongs to both of the poets and neither of them. And returning to Chris's point about the relationship between the reader and the text, I was very interested in making the work a collaboration between not just myself and Chris, but the text and its audience. So that the reader would participate in the process of creating meaning alongside the poets. In this way, that alterity, that otherness begins to speak through the reader as well.*

Talk about the process of making this work, both independently and together. Did you have this intention or develop the idea for a while? What encouraged and/or confounded this (or a book, in general) coming together? What was unexpected or surprising, if anything, about the process? How did it change or evolve?

KMD: *What I enjoy most about collaborations, especially when you're working across long distances, and writing with someone who's in a different geographic space, is the sense of mystery. All that you don't know about your collaborator becomes material for the imaginative work of the book. The collaboration, from my vantage point at least, frames poetry as dialogue, as opposition, as tension. Poetry as the testing of boundaries. Poetry as divination. Poetry as speaking in a third voice, which belongs to both of us and neither of us. We wanted to write together see where this third voice would lead us, how far afield we would find ourselves from our own comfortable practice as individual practitioners. Because we conceived of a conceptual framework, and a governing constraint, from the very beginning, the work came together quite naturally as a chapbook.*

CC: *I'm so used to writing* on the run *but the speed at which this project came together startled me. And I suppose the project as whole startled me, in absolutely thrilling and beautiful ways. Like any correspondence, I felt a responsibility and an accountability toward my recipient, but also the sheer joy of "opening" the letter, whenever I'd see the message's subject blinking in my inbox. The project kind of came together—almost retrospectively— during an encounter with a Spam e-mail's title, which I actually embedded into one of the* poems: "When does a poem stop being yours?" And my endeavor—our endeavor with this co-produced book, I think—was to call into question the ownership of creativity, and to open up a space for multi-user/collaborative authorship.

How did the collaboration process work in the coordination and production of a seamless text wherein there is no obvious distinction between each of your individual voices or production? Was that the intention from the beginning?

KMD: *Absolutely! The best collaborations aren't about the poets as individuals. Denise Duhamel and Julie Marie Wade gave a wonderful interview at* Best American Poetry, *where they talked about collaboration as a kind of collective or shared consciousness. I find their definition entirely compelling. If you ask me, collaboration is about challenging the boundaries between self and other, and interrogating the idea that we can assert ownership over language. When we let go of the arbitrary limitations that we place on language and literary texts, anything becomes possible.*

Did you envision this collection as a collection or understand your process as writing or making specifically around a theme while the poems themselves were being written / the work was being made? How or how not?

KMD: *The chapbook is a ledger, a record, an artifact. It documents the movements of a conversation, its wild associative leaps and driving tensions. In this respect, we envisioned the work as a collection from the very beginning, in the sense that a ledger omits nothing.*

CC: *After a certain point, as we began to understand that this was less of a writing prompt meant to urge us to write—and instead, to write for someone other than ourselves—it became clear that we had a book in our hands.*

What formal structures or other constrictive practices (if any) do you use in the creation of your work? Have certain teachers or instructive environments, or readings/writings/work of other creative people informed the way you work/write?

CC: *This correspondence is certainly indebted to the ideas I continue to formulate around the personal text and especially the irregular, uncategorizable personal text. Much of my work in accounting and accountability has been influenced by Wayne Koestenbaum and his writing and continual mentorship.*

KMD: *Our chapbook was born out of constraint as a way of generating possibility. We decided from the beginning that all poems would be letters, with a timestamp indicating when they were sent. Like a postmark. This gesture ultimately gave the work a sense of urgency and danger, as though we were writing against time, against impending disaster and the destruction of voice and language.*

Speaking of monikers, what does your title represent? How was it generated? Talk about the way you titled the book, and how your process of naming (individual pieces, sections, etc) influences you and/or colors your work specifically.

KMD: *The title was Chris's brilliant contribution, so I'll let him speak about that…*

CC: *Sure, just as I put it in our introduction—invitation?—to readers: a repetition or a reversal; a re: verse in which we correspond lyrically; a re: verse in which our correspondence becomes the poem. So every correspondence, in order to be sustained … needs both repetition and the certain uncertainty of each author's having to rethink their own ideas. These "reversals" are just as important: the moment of disruption which elevates the text above—beyond?—its authors aims or intentions.*

What does this particular work represent to you …as indicative of your method/creative practice? …as indicative of your history? …as indicative of your mission/intentions/hopes/plans?

KMD: *For me, this work represents one of the great possibilities — and one of the great gifts — of collaboration. It invites a spontaneity into one's writing practice, which is something* that's often hard to achieve when working alone. I'm usually a planner when working on a manuscript. But since I never knew what Chris would do next, planning became nearly impossible. Which was great, because I was able to inhabit the present moment more fully when writing. And this spontaneity is something I'll carry with me into my process as an individual creative practitioner.

CC: *Exactly, those reversals I'd mentioned a moment ago. The correspondence goes hand-in-hand with the notebook project I am persistently developing, except in the enactment of actual exchange—hand-in-hand, remember—I had to relinquish my own authority, notions, perspectives, and as Kristina says, relish the immediacy of spontaneous reception and return, a scenario in which I never knew where I was going, or where I would be, only to say that we would be there together.*

To what extent were you working independently or together? How did you go about the editorial process in this case? Were the pieces developed collaboratively from individual texts that started in a different form? Would it be possible to see any part of the process through incremental edits in any way? It could be interesting for the audience to see how a page or pages evolved, how your voices combined, were parsed and edited to become what we see now.

CC: *What's sort of still stunning about this project, for me at least, is how quickly it came together—not just the writing and responding to each other, but in fact the "editing" or "revising" process, which is to say, the whole process didn't take very long at all because it never happened. As I mentioned earlier, I was very conscious of the parameter/reward of writing toward a poetics of accounting/accountability, and with the notebook form in mind, I think it would be both counterproductive but also disingenuous to retrospectively render a correspondence differently, even by "polishing" it. I think the only thing we added before we decided that the manuscript was finished was actually an excision: the omission of our names in each poetic correspondence.*

What does this book DO (as much as what it says or contains)?
CC: *I'm big into the "doing" of a work so I'm appreciative that you framed the question in this manner. The text performs a call and response while signaling the reader toward the exigency of any writing's temporal demands. Because each moment is literally marked, readers are asked to revel in both the immediacy of a response, or alternatively, the space between the messages sent. Each message becomes a charged moment of time, evidence of the time it was written and the broader context in which it occurred.*

KMD: *It suggests, evokes, and invites readers to imagine. I believe that the most powerful and meaningful moments in a text are often the silences. These apertures are what makes room for the reader's imagination. So the text becomes a collaboration between writers, but also, a collaboration between the artists and their audience.*

What would be the best possible outcome for this book? What might it do in the world, and how will its presence as an object facilitate your creative role in your community and beyond? What are your hopes for this book, and for your practice?

KMD: *I hope this book invites conversations with practitioners across disciplines, a dialogue that challenges my aesthetic and pushes me to think through difficult questions about why I write the way that I do.*

CC: *I think the accomplishment of any book is found in its potential integration into other environments, and here I am thinking of the classroom—to be taught, to be discussed, to be repeated and replicated by students and instructors—but even more, areas and avenues distinctly outside of the classroom and academia. The book as a "living object" is explicit here; I'm interested in a book being "useful" only insofar as it's useful for people in whatever way readers and writers choose to approach it.*

Let's talk a little bit about the role of poetics and creative community in social and political activism, so present in our daily lives as we face the often sobering, sometimes dangerous realities of the Capitalocene. How does your process, practice, or work otherwise interface with these conditions? I'd also be curious to hear some thoughts on the challenges we face in speaking and publishing across lines of race, age, privilege, social/cultural background, gender, sexuality (and other identifiers) within the community as well as creating and maintaining safe spaces, vs. the dangers of remaining and producing in isolated "silos" and/or disciplinary and/or institutional bounds?

KMD: *Being a poet is being in a community. And every move we make in language is politically charged. I like to think of poetry as a hypothetical testing ground, where we imagine and refine new ways of structuring communication, relationships, and power dynamics.*

CC: *Sure, I think it's so important—perhaps now more than ever—to get outside of our own isolationist models of socialization and production. While this was not the premise from which we began this project, the co-production of re:verse enabled us to move further and further away from an exclusionary and singular form of authorship.*

Is there anything else we should have asked, or that you want to share?

CC: *I would love for the reader to take this collaboration as a starting point for their own self-inquiries, and to take those questions as a move toward real inter-action: the birth of other poetic correspondences.*

KMD: *Only this: we'd love to hear from you!*

ABOUT THE COVER ART:

The Operating System 2019 chapbooks, in both digital and print, feature art from Heidi Reszies. The work is from a series entitled "Collected Objects & the Dead Birds I Did Not Carry Home," which are mixed media collages with encaustic on 8 x 8 wood panel, made in 2018.

Heidi writes: "This series explores objects/fragments of material culture—how objects occupy space, and my relationship to them or to their absence."

ABOUT THE ARTIST:

Heidi Reszies is a poet/transdisciplinary artist living in Richmond, Virginia. Her visual art is included in the National Museum of Women in the Arts CLARA Database of Women Artists. She teaches letterpress printing at the Virginia Commonwealth University School of the Arts, and is the creator/curator of Artifact Press. Her poetry collection titled *Illusory Borders* is forthcoming from The Operating System in 2019, and now available for pre-order. Her collection titled *Of Water & Other Soft Constructions* was selected by Samiya Bashir as the winner of the Anhinga Press 2018 Robert Dana Prize for Poetry (forthcoming in 2019).

Find her at heidireszies.com

ABOUT THE COLLABORATORS

CHRIS CAMPANIONI is a first-generation American, the son of immigrants from Cuba and Poland, and the author of *the Internet is for real* (C&R Press), which re-enacts the language of the Internet as literary installations. He has worked as a journalist, model, and actor, and he teaches Latinx literature and creative writing at Baruch College and Pace University. His "Billboards" poem that responded to Latino stereotypes and mutable—and often muted—identity in the fashion world was awarded an Academy of American Poets College Prize in 2013, his novel *Going Down* was selected as Best First Book at the 2014 International Latino Book Awards, and his hybrid piece "This body's long (& I'm still loading)" was adapted as an official selection of the Canadian International Film Festival in 2017. A year earlier, he adapted his award-winning course, "Identity, Image, & Intimacy in the Age of the Internet," for his first TEDx Talk. He edits *PANK*, *At Large Magazine*, and *Tupelo Quarterly* and lives in Brooklyn.

WHY PRINT DOCUMENT?

The Operating System uses the language "print document" to differentiate from the book-object as part of our mission to distinguish the act of documentation-in-book-FORM from the act of publishing as a backwards-facing replication of the book's agentive *role* as it may have appeared the last several centuries of its history. Ultimately, I approach the book as TECHNOLOGY: one of a variety of printed documents (in this case, bound) that humans have invented and in turn used to archive and disseminate ideas, beliefs, stories, and other evidence of production.

Ownership and use of printing presses and access to (or restriction of printed materials) has long been a site of struggle, related in many ways to revolutionary activity and the fight for civil rights and free speech all over the world. While (in many countries) the contemporary quotidian landscape has indeed drastically shifted in its access to platforms for sharing information and in the widespread ability to "publish" digitally, even with extremely limited resources, the importance of publication on physical media has not diminished. In fact, this may be the most critical time in recent history for activist groups, artists, and others to insist upon learning, establishing, and encouraging personal and community documentation practices. Hear me out.

With The OS's print endeavors I wanted to open up a conversation about this: the ultimately radical, transgressive act of creating PRINT /DOCUMENTATION in the digital age. It's a question of the archive, and of history: who gets to tell the story, and what evidence of our life, our behaviors, our experiences are we leaving behind? We can know little to nothing about the future into which we're leaving an unprecedentedly digital document trail — but we can be assured that publications, government agencies, museums, schools, and other institutional powers that be will continue to leave BOTH a digital and print version of their production for the official record. Will we?

As a (rogue) anthropologist and long time academic, I can easily pull up many accounts about how lives, behaviors, experiences — how THE STORY of a time or place — was pieced together using the deep study of correspondence, notebooks, and other physical documents which are no longer the norm in many lives and practices. As we move our creative behaviors towards digital note taking, and even audio and video, what can we predict about future technology that is in any way assuring that our stories will be accurately told – or told at all? How will we leave these things for the record?

In these documents we say: WE WERE HERE, WE EXISTED, WE HAVE A DIFFERENT STORY

- Lynne DeSilva-Johnson [ELÆ], Founder/Managing Editor,
THE OPERATING SYSTEM, Brooklyn NY 2019

KRISTINA MARIE DARLING is the author of thirty books, including *Look to Your Left: The Poetics of Spectacle* (University of Akron Press, 2020); *Re: VERSES* (with Chris Campanioni; The Operating System, 2019); *Je Suis L'Autre: Essays & Interrogations* (C&R Press, 2017), which was named one of the "Best Books of 2017" by *The Brooklyn Rail*; and *DARK HORSE: Poems* (C&R Press, 2018), which received a starred review in *Publishers Weekly*. Her work has been recognized with three residencies at Yaddo, where she has held both the Martha Walsh Pulver Residency for a Poet and the Howard Moss Residency in Poetry; a Fundación Valparaíso fellowship; a Hawthornden Castle Fellowship, funded by the Heinz Foundation; an artist-in-residence position at Cité Internationale des Arts in Paris; three residencies at the American Academy in Rome; two grants from the Whiting Foundation; a Morris Fellowship in the Arts; and the Dan Liberthson Prize from the Academy of American Poets, among many other awards and honors. Her poems appear in *The Harvard Review, Poetry International, New American Writing, Nimrod, Passages North, The Mid-American Review*, and on the Academy of American Poets' website, Poets.org. She has published essays in *The Kenyon Review, Agni, Ploughshares, The Gettysburg Review, Gulf Coast, The Iowa Review*, and numerous other magazines. Kristina currently serves as Editor-in-Chief of Tupelo Press and *Tupelo Quarterly*, an opinion columnist at *The Los Angeles Review of Books*, and a contributing writer at *Publishers Weekly*.

SELECTED RECENT AND FORTHCOMING OS PRINT/DOCUMENTS

ARK HIVE-Marthe Reed [2019]
A Bony Framework for the Tangible Universe-D. Allen [kin(d)(*, 2019]
Y - Lori Anderson Moseman
Śnienie / Dreaming - Marta Zelwan/Krystyna Sakowicz,
(Polish-English/dual-language) trans.Victoria Miluch [glossarium, 2019]
Opera on TV-James Brunton [kin(d)(*, 2019]
Alpareghó: Pareil-À-Rien / Alpareghó, Like Nothing Else - Hélène Sanguinetti
(French-English/dual-language), trans, Ann Cefola [glossarium, 2019]
Hall of Waters-Berry Grass [kin(d)(*, 2019]
High Tide Of The Eyes - Bijan Elahi (Farsi-English/dual-language)
trans, Rebecca Ruth Gould and Kayvan Tahmasebian [glossarium, 2019]
I Made for You a New Machine and All it Does is Hope - Richard Lucyshyn [2019]
Illusory Borders-Heidi Reszies [2019]
Transitional Object-Adrian Silbernagel [kin(d)(*, 2019]
A Year of Misreading the Wildcats [2019]
An Absence So Great and Spontaneous It Is Evidence of Light - Anne Gorrick [2018]
The Book of Everyday Instruction - Chloe Bass [2018]
Executive Orders Vol. II - a collaboration with the Organism for Poetic Research [2018]
One More Revolution - Andrea Mazzariello [2018]
The Suitcase Tree - Filip Marinovich [2018]
Chlorosis - Michael Flatt and Derrick Mund [2018]
Sussuros a Mi Padre - Erick Sáenz [2018]
Sharing Plastic - Blake Nemec [2018]
The Book of Sounds - Mehdi Navid (Farsi dual language, trans, Tina Rahimi) [2018]
In Corpore Sano : Creative Practice and the Challenged Body [Anthology, 2018];
Lynne DeSilva-Johnson and Jay Besemer, co-editors
Abandoners - Lesley Ann Wheeler [2018]
Jazzercise is a Language - Gabriel Ojeda-Sague [2018]
Return Trip / Viaje Al Regreso - Israel Dominguez;
(Spanish-English dual language) trans, Margaret Randall [2018]
Born Again - Ivy Johnson [2018]
Attendance - Rocío Carlos and Rachel McLeod Kaminer [2018]
Singing for Nothing - Wally Swist [2018]
The Ways of the Monster - Jay Besemer [2018]

THE 2019 OS CHAPBOOK SERIES

PRINT TITLES:

Vela. - Knar Gavin
[幻] A Phantom Zero - Ryu Ando
Don't Be Scared - Magdalena Zurawski
Re:Verses - Kristina Darling & Chris Campanioni

***

DIGITAL TITLES:

American Policy Player's Guide and Dream Book - Rachel Zolf
The George Oppen Memorial BBQ - Eric Benick
Flight Of The Mothman - Gyasi Hall
Mass Transitions - Sue Landers
The Grass Is Greener When The Sun Is Yellow - Sarah Rosenthal & Valerie Witte
From Being Things, To Equalities In All - Joe Milazzo
These Deals Won't Last Forever - Sasha Amaan Hawkins
Ventriloquy - Bonnie Emerick
A Period Of Non-Enforcement - Lindsay Miles
Quantum Mechanics : Memoirs Of A Quark - Brad Baumgartner
Hara-Kiri On Monkey Bars - Anna Hoff

***

PLEASE SEE OUR FULL CATALOG
FOR FULL LENGTH VOLUMES AND PREVIOUS CHAPBOOK SERIES:
HTTPS://SQUAREUP.COM/STORE/THE-OPERATING-SYSTEM/

THE 2019 SERIES MARKS OUR 7TH AND FINAL SPRING 4-BOOK SERIES
THANK YOU TO ALL THE WONDERFUL CREATORS BEHIND THESE TITLES

CHAPBOOK SERIES 2018 : TALES
Greater Grave - Jacq Greyja; Needles of Itching Feathers - Jared Schlickling;
Want-Catcher - Adra Raine; We, The Monstrous - Mark DuCharme

CHAPBOOK SERIES 2017 : INCANTATIONS
featuring original cover art by Barbara Byers
sp. - Susan Charkes; Radio Poems - Jeffrey Cyphers Wright;
Fixing a Witch/Hexing the Stitch - Jacklyn Janeksela;
cosmos a personal voyage by carl sagan ann druyan steven sotor and me - Connie Mae Oliver

CHAPBOOK SERIES 2016: OF SOUND MIND
*featuring the quilt drawings of Daphne Taylor
Improper Maps - Alex Crowley; While Listening - Alaina Ferris;
Chords - Peter Longofono; Any Seam or Needlework - Stanford Cheung

CHAPBOOK SERIES 2015: OF SYSTEMS OF
*featuring original cover art by Emma Steinkraus
Cyclorama - Davy Knittle; The Sensitive Boy Slumber Party Manifesto - Joseph
Cuillier; Neptune Court - Anton Yakovlev; Schema - Anurak Saelow

CHAPBOOK SERIES 2014: BY HAND
Pull, A Ballad - Maryam Parhizkar;
Can You See that Sound - Jeff Musillo
Executive Producer Chris Carter - Peter Milne Greiner;
Spooky Action at a Distance - Gregory Crosby;

CHAPBOOK SERIES 2013: WOODBLOCK
*featuring original prints from Kevin William Reed
Strange Coherence - Bill Considine; The Sword of Things - Tony Hoffman;
Talk About Man Proof - Lancelot Runge / John Kropa;
An Admission as a Warning Against the Value of Our Conclusions -Alexis Quinlan

DOC U MENT
/däkyəmənt/

First meant "instruction" or "evidence," whether written or not.

noun - a piece of written, printed, or electronic matter that provides information or evidence or that serves as an official record
verb - record (something) in written, photographic, or other form
synonyms - paper - deed - record - writing - act - instrument

[Middle English, precept, from Old French, from Latin *documentum*, example, proof, from *docre*, to teach; see dek- in Indo-European roots.]

Who is responsible for the manufacture of value?

Based on what supercilious ontology have we landed in a space where we vie against other creative people in vain pursuit of the fleeting credibilities of the scarcity economy, rather than freely collaborating and sharing openly with each other in ecstatic celebration of MAKING?

While we understand and acknowledge the economic pressures and fear-mongering that threatens to dominate and crush the creative impulse, we also believe that *now more than ever we have the tools to relinquish agency via cooperative means,* fueled by the fires of the Open Source Movement.

Looking out across the invisible vistas of that rhizomatic parallel country we can begin to see our community beyond constraints, in the place where intention meets resilient, proactive, collaborative organization.

Here is a document born of that belief, sown purely of imagination and will.
When we document we assert. We print to make real, to reify our being there.
When we do so with mindful intention to address our process, to open our work to others, to create beauty in words in space, to respect and acknowledge the strength of the page we now hold physical, a thing in our hand… we remind ourselves that, like Dorothy: *we had the power all along, my dears.*

THE PRINT! DOCUMENT SERIES

is a project of
the trouble with bartleby

in collaboration with
the operating system

www.ingramcontent.com/pod-product-compliance
Lightning Source LLC
Chambersburg PA
CBHW080027130526
44591CB00037B/2702